To Grandmar

Loob on pag
42

Loob on pag 42

from Luke Allen

ANCHOR BOOKS

FROM THE MOUTHS
OF CHILDREN

Edited by

Sarah Marshall

First published in Great Britain in 2003 by
ANCHOR BOOKS
Remus House,
Coltsfoot Drive,
Peterborough, PE2 9JX
Telephone (01733) 898102

HB ISBN 1 84418 146 4
SB ISBN 1 84418 147 2

FOREWORD

Anchor Books is a small press, established in 1992, with the aim of promoting readable poetry to as wide an audience as possible.

We hope to establish an outlet for writers of poetry who may have struggled to see their work in print.

The poems presented here have been selected from many entries, and as always editing proved to be a difficult task.

I trust this selection will delight and please the authors and all those who enjoy reading poetry.

Sarah Marshall
Editor

CONTENTS

SCHOOL
(Dedicated to Mrs Wright)

At school I have:
A n anorak to keep me warm in the playground,
B ooks to note what we have found,
C omputers, so no one has to use writing skills,
D etention, oh the hollers and squeals.
E xcuses, for no homework to give in today,
F rench, to speak in another way,
G eography to learn about different places,
H istory to learn about past faces.
I talian, to learn words from Italy,
J ogging for exercise in PE,
K itching to prepare the dinner,
L unchtime, eating's a winner.
M aths, one, two, three,
N aughty the people we see,
O utside play, where there's yells and play,
P E we do some days.
Q uickly as we go,
R E, a subject we know,
S ports day is fun for me,
T rainers for PE,
U niform is black and red,
V ery smart it could be said,
W ork we produce every day,
X ylophone to bash and play,
Y elling in the playground,
Z zzzz, snoring where children are found!

Teri Manning (11)

GARDENING

Gardening is a lot of fun,
Planting flowers in the sun,
Cutting grass and killing weeds,
Checking on my flower seeds.

Lots of flowers, blue and red,
What a pretty flower bed!
Different flowers all around,
Giving colour to the ground.

Roses, daisies and also heather,
Pampas grass that looks like a feather,
Different colours to catch your eye,
Tall, tall trees that reach the sky.

I like to watch the flowers bloom.
On our mower, we go zoom.
It's very pretty and lots of fun,
But lots of work must be done!

Enfys Evans

THANK YOU

My family help me all year round,
Always there, standing sound.
They help me when I'm in need
And my sister and me they clothe and feed.

My family will look after me, no matter what,
Freezing cold or roasting hot,
Through thick or thin,
I know that together we can win.

My family will look after me at any time,
If I'm in trouble or being blamed for crime,
They're always there, with sound advice,
Being kind and nice.

But once in a while they feel bad,
So I have to be their pad,
But that's what family is all about,
Helping each other out!

Victoria Finlay (10)

MY GRANDAD

My grandad tells me stories with a twinkle in his eye,
Most of them are half the truth, the other half are lies.
He told me of a rocket ship he built when he was young,
He flew it to the Milky Way and landed on the sun.
He said it was really hot, it gave him such a fright,
I said, 'It should have burnt you.' He said he flew at night.
He told me of the places that he and Nan had been,
He told me of the wonders that both of them had seen,
The beauty of the Holy Land and the pyramids of stone
And when they went to Italy, they saw the might of Rome.
They told me of a magic place that he and Nan had been
And of a fairy castle that both of them had seen.
He said that I would see this place that's so big and grand,
He took me to the USA and off to Disneyland.

Lois Rosedale (10)

CROCODILE BUSINESS

A vicar said to the crocodile one day,
'How ever did you get away?'
The croc said, 'From that horrible zoo,
They let me go because I caught the 'flu.'
'Letting you out for a thing like that,
No wonder you're not very fat.'
Croc was waiting for the right time
To gobble up the vicar and say, 'You're mine.'
But that wasn't the end of that,
The vicar was tasty, so was his cat.
When Mr Croc was twenty-one,
He met a young lad called Tom.
After he ate Tom, that was that,
Croc wouldn't eat another man or cat.
To tell you the truth, Tom was really bad,
Croc was sick and going mad.
That wasn't the end of skinny Tom
Because Croc had eaten him all in one.
Tom started to jump, shake and shiver
As he played games inside Croc's liver.
In fact, Tom was having fun
Playing around inside Croc's tum.
One day, Croc tragically died
And poor old Tom was left inside.

Carla Bradley (11)

UNTITLED

If the trees were sweets
And the leaves were cream,
I would spend all day
Licking my dream.

Shameem Adams (6)

MY INVISIBLE FRIEND

My invisible friend is lots of fun,
He jumps and shouts and sings and runs.
He's always doing something wrong,
The other day he sung this song.
It was very mean with naughty words,
My mum was passing and overheard,
She yelled at me and spanked my bum,
As my invisible friend began to run.
He left me there on me tod,
That naughty boy, that little sod.
He visited me the following day,
He apologised, I said OK.
I know he's not the perfect friend,
But our friendship will never end.

My invisible friend is lots of fun,
He jumps and shouts and sings and runs.
He's always doing something bad,
He really is a naughty lad.
But I'm the one that's getting done,
He ain't the one with the throbbing bum.
After all, he can't be seen,
He says we make the perfect team.
He does the crime, I take the rap,
He really is a cheeky chap.
I know he's not the perfect friend,
But our friendship will never end.

Kaylea Simon (14)

EVEN THOUGH

Even though I'm not with you,
We're never apart.
Even though I can't see you,
You've got a place in my heart.

Even though I can't hear you,
You've got a place in my mind.
Even though I can't touch you,
I'll never leave you behind.

Even though they've called you
And you've gone,
In my heart, in my mind,
Your love will shine on.

Hannah Giddings (13)

NEW YEAR'S RESOLUTIONS

Another year's beginning now,
What new things can we do?
Maybe we should eat healthy food,
Or exercise more too.
Especially since at Christmastime
We have piled on a few pounds,
Perhaps we should drink less alcohol,
And cut down on the rounds.

Another year's beginning now,
Which promises will we keep?
Are we going to stop smoking now,
Or will it only last a week?
We know we've tried a million times
And cigarettes have always won.
I'm sure they love to see you suffer,
Why not spoil their fun?

Another year's beginning now,
What resolutions can we make?
Are we going to keep them,
Or will they just be fake?
I wonder if a year from now,
We'll be able to say,
I've kept all of my promises,
What new ones can I make today?

Elizabeth Holt (13)

TWO MAD CATS

Casper and Bambi are completely mad
They are the craziest cats that I've ever had.
They'll wash each other, sweet and calm,
The next minute they'll fight and spit in alarm!
They sleep in the strangest of places;
On the table,
The TV,
Even bookcases!
One time, when Mum walked through the door,
Casper woke up and jumped ten feet off the floor!
Bambi licks your hand, then tries to bite it off!
Casper shoots across the room when you sneeze or cough.
They both love to sleep on rough welcome mats
And that is why they're my two mad cats.

Cassie Brown (15)

A POEM FROM MY SOUL

In my soul I feel my mum and dad,
I feel my friends and my grandad.
I have a person in my heart
And I will always love him.
Even when that person goes, he'll always be with me,
That person is whom I care about so much.
He played with me, he got me a charm,
He made sure I would come to no harm.

My friend did not talk much, but I loved him so,
My heart has a lot of my grandad.
It made me very sad to see him cry when my gran died,
But I know what's in his heart anyway.
My grandad always knew what was best,
But now he doesn't remember anything.
He was a person who could tell my worries,
He was the best a child could ever have.

He lived with me for a while and then went to a home,
He was a present that heaven sent,
Nothing could split me and him up,
No one that lives in this world.
The person who I love so much
Taught me to fight my hates.
He said he always hated fighting,
Even fighting with different religions.

He is my best friend and always will be
And we will never get into trouble.
He is the best and always will be.
He is bored in the home with no one to talk to.
He is as gentle as a lamb and as strong as a lion.
He said he'd wish the world to stop the fighting.

I love him.

Stacy Boal (12)

A HAPPY ENDING

The bride was getting ready,
Brushing her lovely hair.
Everyone could do nothing
But stare.
An hour had gone,
Her groom did not come,
She waited and waited,
She nearly fainted.
She started to cry
And ran out of the church,
The people had followed her
To the silver birch.
She screamed and screamed
And saw her groom,
And saw a knife,
She plunged it slowly
Into her heart,
Making sure they'd
Never part.

Kirri Parks (11) & Nan

IF I RULED THE WORLD

If I ruled the world,
I would call Earth, Cloud 9,
Because everybody would be happy
And the sun would always shine.

If I ruled the world,
Money would grow on trees,
I wouldn't have to pay for anything,
Style icons would get their tips from me!

If I ruled the world,
Everything would be great,
I'd name every single planet in the solar system
After all my bestest mates!

If I ruled the world,
Dreams would become reality,
I'd be rich and famous,
Successful rapper MC!
(Like Ms Dy-Na-Mi-Tee!)

Vickie Brown (14)

IF I RULED THE WORLD

If I ruled the world,
Teachers would wear school uniform,
Buy us chocolate and
Let us chew in class.

If I ruled the world,
Black would be banned
And trainers would
Be made compulsory.

If I ruled the world,
There would be
Only one car per family
And no wasted recyclable products.

There would not be any wars,
No nuclear or chemical weapons.
All guns would be melted
And put to good use.

The poor would be given
The lottery money and
The Queen would share
Buckingham Palace.

Footballers would get paid
For what their job is actually worth
And heart surgeons, nurses, paramedics and
Fire fighters would get more.

If I ruled the world
It would be a better place to live in.
We only have one planet
And I don't want to waste it.

Louise Gamble (16)

What A Mum Is

A mum is there for
Love, support and encouragement.
Is your mum?
My mum is.

A mum is there for
Help, guidance and through the bad times.
Is your mum?
My mum is.

A mum is there for
Kindness, sharing and through the happy times.
Is your mum?
My mum is.

So if these are the qualities of a good mum,
Then I guess my mum is the perfect *mum*.

Carly Ashford (14)

A WINTER POEM

W inter is a cold time,
I ce and frost and snow.
N oses are red and stinging,
T oes and fingers glow.
E verything is still and waiting,
R eady for spring to show.

Anja King (8)

WINTER

W ind whooshing, wind whooshing, wild thunder and lightning
   frighten a little child.

I   'm in bed squeezing my ted, wishing it would be warm instead.

N othing changes, nothing at all, just the sound of a swishing wall.

T wo gloves, a coat, a hat and a scarf, wind wandering through like a
   big draft.

E veryone huggling, snuggling from the storm, they are trying to keep
   nice and warm.

R un away wind, run away home until it's all calmed down to one big
   moan – going, going, *gone!*

Simone Fox (9)

IF I RULED THE WORLD

If I ruled the world,
I would say, 'No war.'
To have a fight
Would be against the law.

If I ruled the world,
It would be like a wonderland,
Blue seas, an orange sun
And beneath our feet brown sand.

If I ruled the world,
Everyone's life would be a success,
The air would be clean
And no one would make a mess.

If I ruled the world,
My aim would be
To make everyone happy
And smile with glee.

If I ruled the world,
You would marry and never divorce,
There would be things that you would do,
But no one would force.

If I ruled the world
I would love every fish,
Every animal, every bird
And grant a special wish.

If I ruled the world,
My thoughts will carry on in others,
Little babies, fathers and kids
And even in mothers.

Isn't it a shame
I don't rule the world?

Emma Taylor (10)

BETTY BOOT AND THE MOUSE!

Betty the boot
Was a hoot
And liked to have lots of fun;
She did funny things
And wanted to sing,
But instead lay about in the sun.

Along came a mouse
Who wanted a house,
Cos his had been trashed by a cat;
He had lived on his own
And had no real home
To which he was really attached.

He passed by a tip
And decided to sit
Thinking he'd better find somewhere to sleep;
He met Betty Boot
And said, 'My, what a hoot!'
And fell down in a hole very deep.

Betty let down a lace
Into this very dark place,
So the mouse could climb all the way up;
He got out of the hole
That had been made by a mole
And found his leg had been awfully cut.

When the wound was all healed,
The mouse revealed,
He wanted to stay in the boot;
So the mouse never went,
Although the boot was battered and bent,
And Betty's still a big hoot.

Sabrina Kelly (10)

MUM AND DAD

They are always there for me,
No matter what I do.
I can always count on them,
They can count on me too.

Who are they, you might say,
Who could be that great?
They are my mum and dad,
Together, my best mates.

Rebecca Clarke (11)

THE WAY OF THE WORLD
(The negative outlook)

The sea is black, the sky is grey
And people suffer every day.
The mists of hate engulf the land,
We'll walk together; but alone we stand.

There is no wrong, there is no right,
There is no day, there is no night.
We don't realise what we have done,
The war is over; no one won.

We're killing ourselves, we're killing each other,
But each woman's our sister, each man our brother,
But before we wipe out our entire race,
May the world come together in a loving embrace.

Lani Irving (12)

WHAT ARE THEY FOR?

Mums, dads, what are they for?
They wash your socks and plenty more.
They're so annoying
And bore you to death,
Nearly anything they say,
You always disobey,
Comes naturally to us seeing as we're all kids,
To cause havoc and fight with your little sis.

Mums, dads, what are they for?
They tell you off and plenty more.
Tidy your room,
Get to bed,
Brush your teeth,
Eat your veg.
I bet you hear this every day,
As they reckon they're perfect in every way.

Mums, dads, I'll tell you what they're for.
They're there to care for you and love you in every single way,
To feed you and teach you whenever they might say.
I know they're all control freaks,
I know that they're all mad,
But all in all I tell you,
They're the best things you'll ever have.

Victoria Strawson (12)

I SPY

Each peach, pear plum,
I spy Tom Thumb,
Tom Thumb in the cupboard,
I spy Mother Hubbard,
Mother Hubbard in the cellar,
I spy Cinderella,
Cinderella up the stairs,
I spy Three Bears,
Three Bears going hunting,
I spy Baby Bunting,
Baby Bunting fast asleep,
I spy Bo-Peep,
Bo-Peep up a hill,
I spy Jack and Jill,
Jack and Jill in a ditch,
I spy the Wicked Witch,
The Wicked Witch in her den,
I spy Three Bears again,
Three Bears still hunting,
I spy Baby Bunting,
Baby Bunting safe and dry,
I spy Plum Pie,
Plum Pie in the sun,
I spy everyone.

Amber Roberts (9) & Sydney Roberts (7)

THE DAY BEFORE CHRISTMAS

While at home, families decorating Christmas trees,
Outside in gardens, snowing.
Friends making snowmen,
Robins eating nuts,
Children tasting snowflakes,
Friends having roast dinner
And children snuggling in bed,
Ready for Christmas Day.

Emma Stafford (8)

WHAT IF?

What if the sky was
A giant blue whale
And each time it laughed,
The world blew a gale?

What if red apples
Ate us instead
And in the day
We would snooze in bed?

What if white rabbits
Would dance and sing
And pretty pink flowers
Would be diamond rings?

What if bats were
Tucked in with delight
And they whispered softly,
'Have a peaceful goodnight'?

Anna Craig (10)

NIGHT

When the moon shines
And the stars go bright,
The spark of light
Shows the lovely sight.

The breeze of wind,
The smell of air
And the shine in the sky
Glows everywhere.

And whenever you seek dark,
Never be scared,
Because the stars' and moon's light
Is everywhere shared.

Anisa Khan (11)

PUNISHMENT

The dark night in which the story lies,
Makes the hearts of those people cry.
When the horrid man came into sight,
He gave those people such a fright.

All was gone, there was nothing left,
As quick as lightning, out he crept.
He spoilt their night, he made his day,
It was probably just God's way.

But what goes around comes around,
At last that night was a gain found.
The horrid man was lying down,
Then he heard a weird sound.

He was pushed down, he had a shock,
Soon the robber broke the lock.
The robber took all the man had,
Which made the man really sad.

He thought, *why do such a crime?*
He forgot what he did last time.

Nabila Khan (12)

SEA HORSE

S uspended in their peaceful, underwater universe amongst the seaweed and coral reef,

E ffortlessly they glide in their unique style as though in another world.

A cting for all the world like living chess pieces, horse-like and majestic.

H idden in the narrow, dark crevices, camouflaged in the shadows.

O ff-shore menaces threaten their fragile environment, potential victims within the ocean.

R elaxing, calm, delicate, their transparent beauty for all to enjoy.

S trong, yet fragile, they dangle in their tranquil surroundings.

E nchanting to watch, they captivate my mind.

Francesca Surrell (10)

DAVID BECKHAM

David Beckham is a star,
His old team mate is Eric Cantona.
He is our captain, he got us so far,
He is England's superstar.
David Beckham has such talent,
No other player is half as gallant.
Brazil, Brazil, they knocked us out,
But David Beckham has no doubt.
Golden Balls is so mint,
He gave Argentina the hint.
David Beckham has a posh car,
He can score from so far.
David can toss a ball,
Just as far as Brooklyn can crawl.
David Beckham and his wife
Do have such a super life.
David's boots don't half flash,
He is getting heaps of cash.
David Beckham eats so healthy,
He is big, strong and wealthy.
David Beckham is the best,
He is better than all the rest.

Daniel Patterson & M Whitwell (11)

THE WRITER OF THIS POEM

The writer of this poem is as
Mischievous as a newborn kitten
With a ball of string,
As helpful as a telephone going
Ring, ring, ring,
As funny as a hyena laughing
In the sand,
As adventurous as a dog
Sniffing the land,
As energetic as a gymnast
On the high bar,
This person comes from afar.
The writer of this poem
Is Daisy Bennett.

Daisy Bennett (10)

O WHAT A DAY

It was a warm, sunny day,
On Saturday the 17th of May.

Me and my dad had to get up,
Because we were going to the FA Cup.

I put on my shirt and got into the car,
We set off very early for we had to travel far.

We got there at 12:00, it was time for lunch,
My dad and I met up with the rest of the Arsenal bunch.

It kicked off at 3:00,
Bergkamp, Vieira, to Oleg Luzhny,
Henry to Wiltord and then to Cole,
1-0 to Arsenal, what a brilliant goal!
First half was almost over when Henry hit the net,
2-0 to Arsenal who had not quite broken sweat.

The second half began and everything looked well,
Seaman to Lauren and forward to Campbell.
Pires took a free kick and boy did the shot bend,
How the opposing team wanted the game to end.
3-0 to Arsenal, o what a day,
Thanks Dad, for great day away.

Toby Wells (9)

SPRING

I remember when buds bloomed,
When birds sang outside my room,
The green grass beneath my feet
And daffodils stood up, so sweet.
That was spring.

Lambs frolicked in the fields,
Baby rabbits turned on their heels,
April showers that swelled the streams
And air that felt so clear and clean.
That was spring.

The morning sun on my face,
I walk the street with quickened pace,
Foals run through the meadows,
All the fawns with the does.
It is spring.

Emma Thomas (9).

HALLOWE'EN

All the sunshine has gone away,
It will come back another day.
The witches' cackle,
The ghosts come out,
All the children scream and shout.

Vampire bats,
Witches' black cats,
Big hairy spiders and scurrying rats.

Hannah Douthwaite (9)

SNOW

I was all alone in the dark
The crisp white snow lay at my feet
It was bitter cold outside
I could hear snow crunching under my feet
I tried to throw a snowball
And touched the soft white snow
It felt cold and sticky
Everything was covered in a white blanket
The wind whistled around me
I could see the birds fluttering in the sky
Then I remembered
I was all alone.

Lauren England (8)

MR WRITE

I ring and she's engaged again,
I know she's talking to him.
She's forgotten me, forgot her friends.
We can't do anything.

I call and can't get through to her,
I've been trying for nights on end.
She thinks I interfere and stir -
It's her heart I'll have to mend.

The line is busy; I'm put on hold.
None of us can stop her.
She pushes me out in the cold.
His picture's in her locker.

I phone and hear the same old tone.
She says that she's in love.
She's going to end up so alone,
He's evil sent from above.

She didn't return all my calls,
She didn't have to go.
He's taken her away from us all
And now I miss her so.

I dial her number and I get through,
It's been three weeks since they met.
She didn't listen when I said
Paedophiles use the net.

Kirsten Burley (16)

THE EXAM

Here we sit in rows of eleven
With only a clock for company
Silently we sit while our life
On a sheet of paper are handed to us
Like a prisoner waiting for a death sentence.
Here we sit in rows of eleven
With the clocks ticking
Getting louder and louder.
It's almost unbearable
In sequence we turn the page,
Answering the questions to our future
Not knowing what we will be getting
In return for our hard work
And back breaking labour.
Here we sit in rows of eleven
While inspectors walk around like prison wardens.
Every time I look at the paper
The words become a swirling whirlpool
Of equations and calculations.
I look up at the clock
And we still have another forty-five minutes to go
Never has time stood still for so long.
Here we sit in rows of eleven
We only have five minutes to go
And we have nearly finished signing our death certificate.
We all wish that we had revised,
Two minutes to go
So we are allowed to put our heavy pens down
And rest our aching hands and brains,
Row by row we march out of our courtroom
After we where let free of our sentences.
There we sat in rows of eleven
We have served our sentence.

Emma Phillips (16)

FICTION

I thought she'd shown me
What love is
Yet, when I looked to the sky
She shot me down and made me cry
These crocodile tears
For deep inside I came to realise our truth.
She told me that I was the one
Her all, the only one in her life
But she dropped me like a tonne
And stabbed me with her knife
To me she was
A dapple light
But turned into a blazing sun
That burnt and singed my eyes
Yet did not blind me from the lies
I could see the wall
That grew between us
Yet not one made
Of brick and mortar
It came to me as no surprise
When you came and told me it was at an end
For I'm looking back
I'm letting go
I'm gone.

Stephen Tuffnell (15)

TUG OF LOVE

You're a bit like a hot country; where the air is so close, it's stifling
But you are my rock, so supportive.
And you remind me of a vice, you've got to unwind to let go
But sometimes I want you to hold onto me.

Screaming for freedom, why can't you appreciate my individuality?
I'm a free spirit, let me fly, I want to flee the nest
But don't let go of me, don't let me fall down, I'll break like glass
I do understand, you don't want to let your little girl go

My God, my God, this is where I need you to carry me
I want to be freed by the chains,
But I think some of them are inside my head
Maybe if I keep getting as angry as I do, I could melt them
Or maybe Mummy and Daddy could hand me the saw.

It's a great big world out there, I know 'cause you keep telling me
I feel like I don't know where my path is, never mind where it leads
If you know where you don't want to go, I suppose it's a start
I love you guys so much, I owe my life to you
And I don't want to hurt you

I know you only nag because you care,
And I appreciate your understanding
I'm not ungrateful,
But I know I make the mistake of taking you for granted
The role of a parent is to make sure
Their child can choose their own paths themselves
I don't think I'll choose the wrong one,
Because of the values you have taught me

You know I hate the feeling of inferiority,
I can't stand to be made a fool of
I'm not stupid; you don't believe it,
But I can look after myself sometimes
The most valuable thing I possess is your love;
I want you to be proud of me
I respect you for your insight through experience;
I want to get my own

It must be so hard to watch your offspring growing up and away
Especially as times have changed since you were kids
My inspiration is that you made it, so I know that I can too
Now you're big kids, and maybe you miss being where I am now.

Katherine Nott (17)

ALL FOR YOU

Blinded by love - naïve, unsure,
each time I saw you, I loved you more.
Not known at first, but then it struck me,
that with you is where I wanted to be.
Your eyes, your smile, everything you do,
your kindness, your care, everything about you.
Every moment spent with you, are memories in my heart,
and I hope the day never comes, when we shall have to part.
You're my heart, you're my soul,
you're my dreams, you're my life,
one day I will be - your ever-loving wife.
I love you so much, and everything I do,
will always and forever, be for only you.

Kate Boud (13)

HORSES

His mane was like fire
His coat like the sun
His hooves like metal
100 miles he could run.

A saddle on his back
A bridle on his head
Any closer and you'd be dead.

Over the hills you may see him run
Blending in with the sun
His hooves like metal
His coat like fire
This is the horse called Messiah!

Tarnya Coulson (11)

WHAT IS PURPLE?

Purple is petals floating in the wind
At autumn time.
Purple is the distant thunderstorm
On New Year's Eve.

Purple is the soft wet paint
That paints the walls.
Purple is the muddy clouds
That might rain on you.

Purple is the sound of the drum
When the band goes past.
Purple is the sound of
The nightclub doors.

Purple is the pretty sunset
In the west
Purple is the moon shining on
The waves as they rush by.

Luke Allen

WINTERTIME

There is a white page of snow waiting for me to draw on it,
I put on my scarf, hat, mitts and my wellies and run outside
And soon there is a picture of footprints on the page,
I look at the lake, it looks like someone has spread sugar over it,
Then I look at the roads, they look treacherous,
Then I add handprints to the picture.
It is getting cold and dark so I decide to go in,
I thought the world had turned sparkly
But the next morning it had all gone.

Ellie O Mantache (8)

HE GOT MAD AND KILLED ME

I entered a writing contest knowing I did my best.
Not knowing that today would be my turn to rest.
I was going down a dirt road no one hardly ever travelled.
It was a dirt road with rocks and gravel.
I looked in my rearview mirror and what did I see?
A strange beat up black car following me.
I saw that the big man had a gun
And I knew that day was the end of my fun.
I kept on driving with tears in my eyes
As I tried to focus on the road and tried not to cry.
He sped up and slowed and sped up again.
As I frantically tried to look for a pen.
I wanted to write, I love you everyone
But on the last word he did what he wanted done.
As he shot me my car lost control
And I hit a tree as it swerved off the road.
They say he got mad because in a car accident he lost his wife.
Now he chose to take someone else's life.
I hope he gets punished for his crime
I think it's only fair that he gets more than just time.
I wish I could have lived another day or two
Just to say all my goodbyes and I love yous.
I wish that day in the future I could see
But now everyone has to live without me.

Shalee Wilcox (14)

I LIKE TO SWIM

My swimming teacher is Paul
And he is very tall,
But best of all
I like to swim!

Paul loves telling jokes
And drinking cans of coke,
But best of all
I like to swim!

Paul is very loud
And if he taught a champion to swim for England
He would be very proud
But best of all
I like to swim!

Paul doesn't like to wait
And talks to his invisible mate,
But best of all
I like to swim!

Paul taught me from the age of six
And gave me all his swimming tips,
But best of all
I like to swim!

But now I'm ten
And I can beat all the men,
But best of all
I know I can swim!

Rebecca Hiorns (10)

POWER PEOPLE RULE OUR WORLD

The world never stops.
Like a balloon that never pops,
Ever growing, new people, new places, new things to see,
That's my opinion only me.

Power people rule our world.

Another thing people die,
The relatives, stand and cry,
People with no feelings that's who I hate,
For them, the never opening Heaven's gate.

Power people rule our world

Throughout the world wars are happening,
It's a never-ending thing,
On the battlefields cries are heard,
You'd think the leaders were absurd.

Power people rule our world.

The police just stand and stare.
Their weapons just cause a flare.
Huge helmets, guns, shields and knives,
It puzzles me how people survive.

Power people rule our world.

Madeline Dell (12)

TEACHERS

'Where's your homework?'
'Try it again!'
'Caution card, *now!*'
'Wash off that stain!'
No, wait,
Teachers aren't *all* that bad.
In fact, if I didn't have teachers,
I would be mad!
'You can have a merit!'
'Excellent work, that's good!'
'This is very neat!'
'You've done as well as you could!'
That's more like them,
You see, teachers at my school,
Are not bad at all,
In fact, they're quite cool!

Mrinalini Dey (12)

KIDS ON BIG KIDS

I go to school with my hair gelled and my shirt hanging out,
I meet my friends,
My mum shouts, 'Bye Arif.'
What am I to do?

I forget to take my swimming kit
I don't mind
My mum arrives at the school,
What am I to do?

I go to rugby on Saturday, I try my best,
I get all dirty,
My mum shouts, 'Arif you're a bam!'
What am I to do?

My friend sends me a text message
My mum reads it,
And then sends what she thinks is a witty reply,
What am I to do?

Mums are very strange, always fussing over you,
I get quite embarrassed
I wouldn't be without her though,
What am I to do?

Arif Khan (13)

KIDS ON BIG KIDS

My mum is called Joyce,
She goes to Robert Gordons University,

My mum is older than most of the other students,
She wants to be an accountant,

My mum likes to phone Kaz and Val,
She speaks for a long time,

My mum takes the dogs out at night-time,
She also takes them to the moors,

My mum has blonde hair and blue eyes,
She wears big hoop earrings,

My mum is the best person in the world,
She looks after us and we love her!

Hannah Khan (9)

KIDS ON BIG KIDS

I have a football coach called Gordon,
We train on Friday and a match on Sunday,

He is very kind and he doesn't shout,
At the end of training he lets us play,

We had our first match last week,
I tried my best to score a goal,

It was very hard since I am only seven,
I tried my best, but I only hit the pole.

Samir Khan (7)

LIVING BY THE GROWN UPS' RULES

Grown ups always know what to do,
But really they haven't got a clue!
Teachers try to fill my mind,
But now I've sussed the learned kind.
My parents think they know what's best,
It's time I put them to the test.
I'm me in my own right,
I'm fed up of having to fight!
To kick back at the system,
I ask myself, would I miss them?
If all the adults were wiped out,
I'd have to start to fend for myself.
Would I party on 'til late?
Or would I be tucked in bed by eight?
How does it feel to be big like you?
Three more years I'll be a grown up too!

Hannah Taylor (15)

TEACHERS, TEACHERS

Teachers, teachers
They say anything,
They say, 'Do your work,
Face the front.'
Teachers, teachers
They say, 'Have manners.'
They say, 'Walk nicely.'
They say, 'Go downstairs.'
Teachers, teachers
What will they say next?
Teachers, teachers,
What will they say next?

Arinola Lawal (9)

NICE THINGS

The smell of bacon cooking in the pan,
The deep refreshing breeze,
A twinkling dragonfly hovering in the air,
The tall, magnificent trees.

A big, white horse neighing in the field,
The scent of warm, fresh bread,
The powdery white snow sitting on a mountain,
The birds flying overhead.

A crunchie cookie from the oven,
A prawn and mayonnaise bread roll,
Marzipan fruits in a pretty box,
A small, white China doll.

Little dogs that bark in the night,
A Chinese takeaway,
The juicy apple sprinkled with sugar
And a lovely sunny day.

Rachel Lisk

KIDS ON . . . BIG KIDS

My mum's the utter best,
She passes the 'great mum' test,
She gives me into trouble for being a nutter,
But I don't blame her,
Because I love her.

Emma Ritchie (11)

GONE WITH THE WIND

Gone forever, never coming back
Like a bird in the wind, her wings have flapped.
In the house of the Lord is where she did pray
Till that fatal night when it was where she lay.

To think of happy times that we did have
And to know that they are never coming back
Brings great sadness to my world
The thoughts in my head twirl and swirl.

I need release from the arms of this living Hell
I need to feel happy and know that all is well
But living without her hurts me so bad
Half of me is missing and will never come back.

We were very close and her death's made me sad
I am not myself, my world's rotten - gone bad
But still I live on this misery
And face each day being unhappy.

To say this is hard is an understatement
I need some reassurance but nothing helps
I can never move on - just live on with my mind bent
Forever she is gone not worrying how I've felt.

On Christmas Day - I will never forget
This tragedy - like cement - did set
And so her life is no more to be
I'll always love you Gran - RIP.

Victoria Taylor (14)

MY FAVOURITE TEACHER

All my teachers to date,
Have been kind and really great.
But the one now is the very best,
In my opinion a cut above the rest.
She looks young and isn't very tall.
In fact, petite and very small.
Kind and caring but very strict.
Has full control without a stick.
She makes learning interesting and fun.
Always checks we understand what we've done.
With her around, school is a pleasure.
Memories of her, I'll always treasure.

Gemma Roberts (11)

OWL

I am swift as the wind,
Quiet as the ocean,
Watchful as a mother,
Like poetry in motion.

Smarter than a fox,
Wiser than the trees,
So cunning and clever,
I bring the world to its knees.

I sleep by day,
But oh, by night,
I slaughter my prey,
With next to no fight.

I am so wise,
So clever, so sly.
For if knowledge is power,
Then a god am I.

Nicola Collins (12)

HAPPINESS

Happiness swiftly flows down my body,
as if it was air.
I feel good like a feather
flowing through the night sky.
Anger is hot and happiness is cold,
every day the cold rises
and soon I will freeze with happiness.
Happiness makes me want to smile
in the graceful wind,
it makes me feel like a ray of sun,
shining on everyone
and making them happy.
Happiness sounds like laughter and joy,
you may not see it but you can feel it
and hear it all around you.
I wish everyone could have happiness every day
because happiness is like water,
we can't live without it.

Timothy Martin Wood (10)

IF I RULED THE WORLD . . .

If I ruled the world, money would grow on trees,
There would be no school, just lots of shopping sprees.
Gucci, Versace, Armani, D&G,
Lots of designer labels for me, me, me!

If I ruled the world, everyone would be mates,
All the girls and boys would go on lots of dates.
If I ruled the world, the cinema would be free,
To see all the films there could possibly be.

If I ruled the world, there would be no war,
If I ruled the world, there would be no poor.
If I ruled the world, I'd get everyone together,
And make a toast to the best ruler ever!

Children would play all day long,
Musicians would write the best ever song,
Teenagers would never get in a mood,
Parents and adults would never be a prude.

MPs wouldn't talk about boring events,
I'd made a day devoted to scouts and their tents.
Husbands would never moan about their wives
And murderers would never kill, not even with knives.

Toddlers would never eat all those worms,
And I'd ban whoever invented the curly perms!
I'd make weekends to buy make-up and lots of clothes,
And all depressed people wouldn't be on all time lows.

I'd make all creepy crawlies not look so scary,
And all those old men not look so hairy!
I'd invent a robot to do all the cooking and cleaning,
That would leave lots of faces definitely beaming.
So if I ruled the world, now you can see,
How good the world could possibly be!

Laura Smyth (14)

GUESS WHO?

These people are master villains,
Who plot their evil plans,
To outlaw all our cool stuff,
With their stupid bans.

They kill us all with classwork,
And then with homework too,
And if you can't manage to do it,
Then you've got a detention to do.

Have you had a guess yet?
Who these people are?
Who every weekday morning
Try to run you over in their car?

It's teachers.

Stefanie Harris (14)

MY GRAN

My gran was the greatest
She really was the best
She loved playing games
However daft they were
She loved to give me cuddles
Even when I was bad
She was my very special gran
She really loved to make me laugh
She once giggled so much she peed her pants
Her cheeks went red when she drank
She was old in looks
But so young at heart
We all knew that, but then she died
I cried and cried
All day and night week after week
Now ever tear has fallen
What is left, people ask
Our love for each other is all I need
Because she is, was and always will be
My very lovely gran.

Heidi Carter

MOUNT VESUVIUS

Sitting there quietly waiting
Nature's own great lion
But then it starts to growl and rumble
And lets out a giant roar
People start to run away
But the lava reaches them
Then it starts to burn their flesh
And hardens them to stone
Roaring, rushing, demolishing everything
The heat is burning, the smell is awful
The spectacle of amazing light
Has such amazing power
All is silent now
But everything is gone
Not even a blade of grass shows
Against the blackened ground
The people came back to the city
To find there's nothing left
They go to where their houses stood
Not even a brick left standing
Oh how I wish this didn't happen
Big, great Mount Vesuvius.

Christina Scott (11)

ANGEL ON A STAR

One very special angel I'm proud to say I know,
Wraps her wings around me when I'm feeling low.

Whatever makes me cry, she always seems to care.
Her halo isn't visible but I can tell it's there.

And when I feel alone at night I know just where she'll be.
Sitting on her star, high up with the moon, winking at me.

She takes my deepest secrets and locks them all away.
She sprinkles them with stardust and helps the burden lay.

There's magic; a youthful wisdom held within her eyes;
'What are we going to do?' she says, smiling and sighs.

She can't be with me all the time but I know she's never far.
When she leaves and says goodbye, she goes back to her star.

This angel's my English teacher; she bares a heart rare.
I know she's not mine but I know she's always there.

Heather Stirling (15)

ANNIE AND BILL

My grandparents make me laugh
Wake me up at seven and plonk me in the bath.
Have me ready for eight o'clock
Tidy my uniform, pull up my sock.
They fall out like Tom and Jerry
Both then turn as red as a berry.
My grandma's a good cook
She bakes cakes without a book.
My grandad watches telly whilst reading the paper
He really is a daft old caper.
They buy me sweets and give me pocket money
But best of all they gave me my mummy!

Hannah Troy (9)

HE'S ALRIGHT REALLY, DAD

Tidy your bedroom
That's what is said
I say something cheeky
He says get to bed
And yet I still love him
Though not when he's mad
But, when I think about it
He's alright really, Dad.

He maybe sarcastic
But then, so am I
And sometimes he does get
That weird look in his eye
But he helps me through all
The good and the bad
And when I think about it
He's alright really, Dad.

When I ask for anything
He, straight away thinks of money
And most things he said
Are just down right funny
But I'm lucky I have him
And most days I'm glad
And I just can't help thinking
I love him, my dad.

Megan Connelly (14)

WHAT'S HAPPENED TO THE WORLD TODAY?

What's happened to the world today?
What's happened to our minds?
Murder, drugs, we bathe in it,
What's happened to our time?

What's happened to the world today?
Why do we act like this?
Stealing, racism, we pump and pump,
Why do we do these things?

What's happened to the world today?
Who do we think we are?
Kidnapping, rape, we thrive in it,
Who gives us this right?

What's happened to the world today?
How can we be so cruel?
Bombs, shootings happen everyday,
How can we live like this?

What's happened to the world today?
When will we kill these things?
Terror, war, we're breeding it,
When will it ever stop?

Helen Scholey (14)

IF I RULED THE WORLD

If I ruled the world,
I'd make sure there would be,
An end to hunger
And to poverty.

If I ruled the world,
I'd make sure that we saw,
An end to violence
And to war.

If I ruled the world,
Friendships would last,
And hurt and homelessness,
Would be a thing of the past.

Everyone together,
Joined hand in hand,
Not divided as we fall,
But united as we stand.

Stefanie Harris (14)

IF I RULED THE WORLD

If I ruled the world
I'll think about the nature first
All the beautiful flowers
Dug away in the construction's dirt
I'll also make a special place for animals
No more cages, gates or barbed wires
No more cruelty to animals
No more stuff to guard them from freedom
Animals should be free like wild fire
Now you know that, the world would be great
If I was in charge
But the first thing I would need to do
Is to rule state by state.

Sheun Oshinbolu (10)

UPSIDE DOWN

How would it be to be upside down?
Looking at things from a different angle
Keep moving around in a small rectangle
I wonder what it would be like.

How would it be to be upside down?
Having the world turned around
There is no need for the ground
That is what it would be like!

Niresha Umaichelvam (9)

A SMILE

How do you smile,
To not look vile,
A funny wit, usually does it,
For people like you,
Now for me, it doesn't work.

How do you smile,
To not look vile,
A sense of adventure, usually does it,
For people like you,
Now for me, it doesn't click.

How do you smile,
To not look vile,
A good book, usually does it,
For people like you,
Now for me, it doesn't stick.

How do you smile,
To not look vile,
To look at my sister, for a while,
Usually does it for me,
For people like you,
It doesn't do!

Indresh Umaichelvam (12)

WHAT WILL I BE FOR HALLOWE'EN?

Maybe I'll be a clown
Or a queen wearing a gown
Maybe I'll be a snake
What will I wear then? Oh heck!

Maybe I'll be a fairy
But wait, that's not scary!
Maybe I'll be a bat
Or a fierce black cat!

What about a rag doll?
Or a princess from the ball
Or how about a wicked witch?
Wait! I'll be a monster from the ditch!

Now I'll think long and hard
About what I will be
My parents say I don't need a costume 'cause
I got a good one . . . *me!*

Laura Douglas (10)

MY WISH

My wish could never be,
I want my family to stay with me,
To never die,
Then I wouldn't cry,
For evermore,
Their kisses to store
A peck upon my cheek,
To have every day,
Not a mere remembrance,
Of what they used to say,
I love everyone so much,
I know their soft, warm touch,
Every second, every minute, every hour,
My family give me the power,
I love them,
I love the times we laugh,
I love the times we cry,
I hate it when they die.
Some have been,
Some still to come,
But when they go,
I need them to know,
How much I love them.

Sharna Holman (12)

4005

If I ruled the world . . .
I would make people see sense,
And stop throwing rubbish on the ground
To help keep our world clean,
With recycling and rubbish bins all around.

If I ruled the world . . .
I would reduce the prices for *everything!*
I would ban cats,
With their twitching noses and evil eyes,
And make MPs wear outrageous hats.

If I ruled the world . . .
I would declare that schools don't open on Mondays,
To stop us kids getting Monday blues,
I would ban homework and school uniform,
And not have to learn things that we won't ever use!

If I ruled the world . . .
I would stop people from being so mean,
Keep Earth peaceful and friendly
Stop the attacks and wars
And make *my* world the best place to be

If I ruled the world . . .
I would stop the ice from melting,
To keep those there alive
And cool down the ozone layer
To help Earth see 4005.

Isabel Smith (14)

ADULTS

I am a child,
Who is expected to be mild.
But when grown-ups get in my way,
There is a lot that I can say.

'Do your homework,' they will say,
'Don't leave it till another day.
Eat up all your carrots and peas,
'They're good for you,' they will tease.

'Do this . . .
Do that . . .
Feed this fish,
Brush the cat.
Do this . . .
Do that . . .
Will you stop being such a brat!'

But on the other hand . . .
I'd have to say,
They look after me every day.
They give me sweets and toys too,
So I think they're okay!
What about you?

Melissa Redrup (12)

THE STAGECOACH

Trotting briskly through the cobbled streets,
In Stamford the past and present meets,
Snorting, sweating, the dapple greys lead the way,
Down the hill and onto the George, where they will rest and stay.

The smell of creaking leather and velvet curtains,
Drawn back to show us for certain.
The black top hats, hooded cloaks and waistcoats
And ladies dressed in their best.

This is the way it used to be,
In the olden times long before me,
Before the bus, the train, the plane and the car,
Travelling by stagecoach near and far.

Olivia Adams (10)

WINTER WONDERLAND

Snow gleaming on the path,
Myself engulfed in an icy wrath,
Miserable trees with branches bare,
Late at night they are spooky and do scare.

This is how many see the winter scene,
But I see it, within my eye a gleam,
For in my mind, Christmas is here
And with it, the usual jolly cheer.

Dressed up in gloves, a scarf and a hat,
What would those misery guts say about that?
The old tradition of Christmas song,
A tradition that has lasted for so long.

So now that winter is at last here,
Give it a smile, if not a cheer,
For winter is a time of fun,
Even if there is not much sun.

Stacey Ingram

STRANDED

Look at you standing there on that rock,
You stupid girl you're stranded now, all blocked off
She told you, you should go, you said, 'No, wait a mo,'
So she did, look where that got you,
Stranded on a rock.

You could see the tide was coming in
How come you always end up in danger
It's like you're a disaster ready to pop out
And get yourself stranded
You start to panic as you realise you're in danger.

Strong currents, washful waves
Tears running on your mate's face,
Crowds forming, tension rising
Dramatic atmosphere surrounds you both
Stranded on a rock.

The lifeboat's on its way to rescue you both
Hurry, you thought, almost falling off the edge
As the force of the current attacked your legs
Rows of waves tackled both your knees
Noises in the background seemed to get louder
The bear's back is where you got stranded
It's where all the strong currents are landed.

The boat was there, a man jumped out into the sea
Rushing both of you into the boat
Like a shooting star, as quick as lightning
No minute to waste
You're safe now, alive but cold
Stay away from the beach for good is what you got told.

Nicole Slater (15)

FEAR

Fear is the black that sends shivers
    down my back
Fear tastes like the slime that slugs
    leave behind
Fear smells like dung that's been
    out in the sun
Fear looks like ghosts all creepy
    and gross
Fear sounds like thunder getting
    louder and louder
Fear feels like maggots all
    crawling and white
But most of all
    fear fills me with fright.

Andrew Mitchell (10)

DERBY DAY AT LAST

(A poem about Sheffield United FC)

It's derby day at last
Rival fans come rushing past
Proud to wear the red and white
What a beautiful sight!
All they want at the bottom of their soul
Is a simple goal.

Pacy players on the wing
From the bottom of our hearts
We can't help but sing
From the wing a perfect ball
Straight to the strikers all so tall
Fans munching pies
The real *fans* not afraid to cry.

From up on high the lane chants
The opposition fans looking like ants
We will rule for evermore
Above the rest we will soar
United.

Daniel Hall

MY MAGIC BOX
(Inspired by 'Magic Box' by Kit Wright)

I will put in the box . . .
A leaping spark from an electric fish,
A smooth shell from the seaside,
The sparkling fireworks in the night sky.

I will put in the box . . .
The fresh ice-cold snowflakes on a winter's day,
The sizzling, sunny beaches,
The Egyptian pyramids.

I will put in the box . . .
A dolphin swimming joyfully,
Some delicious ice cream,
Loads of Christmas presents.

Maria-Luisa Gigova (10)

A MEGA, MONSTER COLD

Accompanied by your stomach,
Your head beats out a rhythm
As your earache does the conga
With your warm, sweaty palms.
You moan with frustration
As your body doesn't listen,
When you tell it to behave
And take some Aspirin.
Now your belly starts to bubble
And you think you're gonna blow,
Till you puke out the Aspirin
And spend hours on the bog.
Now you're recovering slowly,
As brain takes control.
'What the hell was that,' you say,
A mega, monster cold!

Emily Allen (12)

ANIMAL FEATURES

A fish is scaly with big fat lips,
You can't see its bottom cos it's got no hips.

A cat is soft like cotton wool,
They're really cute and totally cool.

A dog is nice to have around,
The way they always sniff the ground.

Now a tiger really would be fun,
But I wouldn't want to live with one!

Laura Emily Reed (12)

REALITY

Where is reality?
Where is the road to home?
Reflections of light,
Reflections of rays,
Where is your password
That you have never heard?
Can you not see?
Is this just a part of me?

Where is reality?
Where is the road to home?
We are all just born,
Who made this world?
For us to believe,
Every single heart is down,
Every little child is lost,
Show me the way,
Oh Lord.

Let me touch your hearts,
Let me feel your pain,
Let me soothe your brain,
Let me just for once,
Touch - reality.

A Bhambra

THE ENVIRONMENT

The environment should be a wonderful place
where children play and animals are safe
world fell apart as years went by
but hopefully one day it will be
a super place for you and I.

Gemma McGowan (14)

MY PERFECT DREAM

In my perfect dream
There is a world that I can eat
That tastes so sweet
And perfectly light in an ever dark street

In my perfect dream
There would be no war
And killing stops right there
In the real world

In my perfect dream
There is peace in every corner of every street
And when the night comes
There is no evil to haunt my dream

In my perfect dream
There is a world that lives forever
With no war and no killing
And lots of food to eat

In my perfect dream
Animals are fairly treated
And not kicked out on the street
And left to die in the snow and sleet

This is my perfect dream
And no one can take it away from me
And no one else can keep it
No one but me!

Louise Day (13)

WHAT HOMEWORK MISS?

'What homework Miss?
I didn't know that!
My cat chewed it up on the bestest mat.'

'Was it due in today?
Oh I've got a note.
My brother dropped something on it yesterday.'

'Oh that homework Miss!
My brother lent forward to give me a kiss
But unfortunately he dribbled on this.
Me he missed!'

'I couldn't hand in this one, I'm sorry.
It fell out of my hands and went under a lorry.'

'I'll hand it in tomorrow Miss,
I really do promise.
There's only one problem Miss,
I lent it to my friend Morris.'

'Oh look, she's got it, look at this.'
And the crowd shouted yippee.
'Oops, I'm really sorry Miss,
That's for history.'

Roseth Nkosi (12)

A Child's Dream

An angel tapped me on the shoulder one day,
believe me, I felt it,
whispered in my ear, I couldn't have dreamt it,
he said, 'Look back, remember so long ago,
it's all there in your memory, what you think you don't know.'

And for a second I knew and I really could see it,
that happiness is and always would be it.
And that bad times mean nothing,
and aren't even real,
and that Heaven is everything good you can feel.

He said when I closed my eyes,
I can always recall,
what my head says means nothing, but my heart knows it all,
if I tried I'd remember, it's all there in my heart,
and we're always together and we never will part.

Lucie King

MY DADDY

I miss my dad,
He misses me,
I miss my dad,
I miss sitting on his knee.

I miss my dad,
I know he cares,
I miss my dad,
Taking me to bed, upstairs.

I miss my dad,
I love him too,
I miss my dad,
He's like a good shoe.

I miss my dad,
Oh, where is he?
I miss my dad,
Where can he be?

Anastasia Pepsi Tasou (9)

BULLY

I've never been a bully,
So I suppose I don't understand fully
Why a bully wants to be a bully,
But don't find it very funny.

The girl next door is a bully,
Her name is Jackie Scully,
She thinks she's funny,
I think she's silly!

Jackie Scully,
She finds it funny to hit and call,
The other girls a twit!
I still don't understand fully,
Why she wants to be a bully.

One day Jackie Scully will get hit back!
When the day comes I'll sit back and think
Maybe next time
Jackie Scully will think twice.

Victoria Furber (10)

SCHOOL!

In the morning school is boring,
In the afternoon you wish you could go soon,
You listen for the bell,
Then you run like hell!
Your teacher wants you back for detention.
You pay no attention!

It's a mystery how you got through history,
You go for lunch in a bunch,
Crisps and sweets!
Then back down the school streets,
But there are no treats
And it's so uncool!
Cos you're back at school!

Megan Furber (15)

SNOW

It's snowing again, isn't it nice?
We're slipping and sliding on the ice.
That freezes beneath the blanket of cold,
White fresh flakes that soon grow old.
Then, as it melts, a horrible slush
Gets in your way, you dare not rush.
Down the road to the shop to buy
A new sledge . . . too late, goodbye!

Bethany Becconsall (10)

CANDLES

Candles are yellow and red,
they light up at night.
Candles make shadows,
candles are so bright.

Candles are different sizes,
straight, round and tall.
Circular, wonky
and sometimes they are small.

Candles are purple and blue,
gold, white and cream.
In the night you light a candle
and you can dream.

Megan Cann (7)

THE PLAYGROUND

At night the playground comes alive,
From the spooks having a ball
Looking for humans,
To see the one who falls.

Watch out, they're about,
The one who falls is you,
Girl ghosts put on their best dress,
While boy ghosts wait to say, 'Boo!'

The night goes on,
Spooks are still at the ball,
Vampires clean their teeth,
Waiting in the cool.

The spooks fade away,
The playground day's done,
You're the fool who fell,
They make no sound.

Hannah Clissett (10)

LUKE THE LION

Once lived Luke the lion, he lived in a cave
All his friends said he was very brave.
But one day he was nasty to all his friends
In their friendship there were twists and ends.
One day Sammy squirrel was eating a nut
It fell and hit poor Luke in the gut.
Luke the lion was extremely mad
He was going to get Sammy real bad.
All the next day he stayed up that tree,
Even if he needed to pee.
He aimed it at a tree down below
He said, 'I don't care, it will help the trees to grow.'
Sammy left a note to say, I'm sorry for yesterday,
The letter was sweet and polite
But it wasn't to the lion's delight.
He waited till it was pitch dark
Till he heard the wolves' fierce bark
Luke saw him by the tree
And then he counted 1, 2, 3.
Luke jumped out and grabbed his prey
I'll have that for my supper today.
Sammy the squirrel bit the big one,
Now Sammy the squirrel is all one.

Stephanie McGarry (10)

YOUTH AND OLD AGE

Old age and youth
Cannot live together.
Youth is full of cheer,
Age is all aches,
Youth like a spring daffodil swaying in the breeze,
Age like an autumn leaf turning from soft to crisp.
Youth is stacked with energy,
Age is hard to hide.
Youth is majestic,
Age is fantastic.
Youth is bold and sometimes cold,
Age is a tea cosy kept warm and dry.
Youth is a big adventure,
Age is bigger yet.
Age is the dreadful feeling of getting old,
Youth is the excitement of another birthday.

Amie Garforth (11)

MY MUM

I love my mum so dear and sweet,
When I'm good, I sweep her off her feet.
I give her hugs, I give her kisses
At parents' evening she talks to Misses.
I'm worried but she comes to say,
'You take Miss's breath away.'
At last you see my mum is kind,
I'd never leave my mum behind!

Natalie Hines (10)

THE STREETS

Hi, I'm Billy, I live on the street
If I don't do as I'm told
I'm sure to get beat.
I live in the corner of Highway Road
I'm as dirty and as smelly
As a forty year old toad.

I don't have much water
I don't have much food
I'm always very cold at night
But I'm never in a mood.

I wish someday to live in a house
Where people would take some care
I could have a bed and a family
And nobody would stare.

So that is me, Billy the street kid
Whose dreams are far away,
I'd love to live in a house
Someday Billy, someday.

Laura Probert (12)

WHAT IS GOING ON?

Once would the oaks stand strong and tall
And the eagles that would land on its firm branches and call.
Once where some deer would run
Now there's just an airport, not much fun!
I remember when the birds would fly,
Now there's just a runway, why?
I remember the seeds I planted to grow,
Now none of them are going to show!

James Wareing (9)

SPRING

Spring is when the leaves start growing on the trees.
Spring is when we start seeing bees.
Spring is when the flowers start to bloom
And when caterpillars come out of their cocoons.
So get ready for when spring is over
And I start to walk my dog Rover
Through the woods and over the clover.

Imaan Khan (10)

THE DOG NEXT DOOR

The dog next door is just a pup
but through the fence she can climb up.
Barking day and night I hear
I wish it would just disappear.
She has a coat of black and white
but don't come close for she may bite.
So as she watches me go by
it looks as if she's going to cry.
Don't get me wrong, she's not that bad
but the noise she makes drives me mad.

Martin Watt (12)

DAYBREAK

It's the weekend and morning has come,
everything has just begun.
I see birds outside feeding their young,
people are getting up and people are still sleeping,
but all I know is that I'm not weeping.
I might go to the cinema or I might not,
because I think my parents might have forgot.
But I don't care because I'm not in despair,
it is just me, my parents and my sister,
but I better be careful this weekend,
because last weekend I got a blister.
So goodbye for now and I'll see you soon,
because probably next time I'll talk about a cocoon.

Omar Khan (14)

MY PIZZA

I was sat on the couch, my stomach started to groan
when I shouted to my dad, get on that phone!
While he was ringing the pizza man's number
I thought I'd just die that minute, of great hunger.
But the knock on the door just made my mouth water
Not to have pizza would be complete torture!
With pepperoni, chilli and ham
I like mine with extra lamb.
The worst of all is lots of veg
They send my tastebuds over the edge.

That was my pizza for tea.

Harry Hedley (9)

THE VALLEY OF DREAMS

In a place of myth and fantasy,
Pounding drums fill the sky,
In a land of dreams and imagination,
Why bother to ask why?
Why not have a black sun,
Moving across a silver sky
Why not have a golden lake,
Why bother to ask why?

In a city made of light and shadow,
Both life and death walk the roads,
A time where things that are,
Are things that shall be,
And things that have happened,
No human shall ever see
A time . . . where things that shall never happen . . .
Will forever come to be,
And the things that shall not happen,
Yesterday . . . we shall see.

In a place of myth,
Animals roam the sky,
In a place of myth,
Nobody asks why?
In a place of myth,
Where trees and rocks fly,
In a valley of dreams,
Pounding drums fill a silver sky.

Sam Sherratt (11)

ACCIDENTS HAPPEN, SOMETIMES!

There was a crash,
My head was nearly smashed,
I was in a bad position,
The doc said I was in a serious condition,
I suddenly woke,
I could smell smoke,
They were lifting me up,
A man gave me a cup,
Drink this he said,
I was in a bed,
Smoke was coming from the two cars,
I saw two people carrying candles in jars,
The ambulance's doors shut,
A doctor was now looking at my cut,
I longed to see my parents, where were they,
And my sister Fay.
I was really scared, I was all alone,
I heard someone on a phone,
There was a tap on my shoulder,
Then my hand was being held by a hand much colder,
I was in my bed at home,
I was handed a scone,
It was my mum,
This is dumb,
Said my sister Fay,
It was a new day,
It was all dreamed,
My mum said I had screamed,
But it was only a dream!

Cherry Watson (11)

As I Walk Along The Street

As I walk along the street
I hear a drum beat.

As I walk along the street
The bee stings my feet.

As I walk along the street
I am very neat.

As I walk along the street
There's lots of wheat.

As I walk along the street
There's lots of things to eat.

As I walk along the street
I can feel the heat.

As I walk along the street
I see a brand new seat.

As I walk along the street
I see a treat.

As I walk along the street
I see my friend Pete.

As I walk along the street
I eat a sweet.

As I walk along the street
I see some meat.

As I walk along the street . . .

Grace Bellwood

MIDNIGHT JUNGLE

The tigers are growling,
The bears are prowling,
The cheetahs are running,
The birds are humming,
All in a midnight jungle.

The trees are bustling,
The plants are rustling,
The parrot is singing,
The monkeys are swinging,
All in a midnight jungle.

The dolphins are diving,
The chameleons are disgusting,
The elephants are strolling,
The lions are patrolling,
All in a midnight jungle.

The zebras are drinking,
The giraffes are blinking,
The lynxes are pouncing,
The frogs are bouncing,
All in a midnight jungle.

The crocodiles are eating,
The hippos are fleeting,
The lions are threatening,
The wildebeest are beckoning,
All in a midnight jungle.

The spiders are crawling,
The whales are bawling,
The apes are drowning,
The pumas are frowning,
All in a midnight jungle.

Amy Brenndorfer (9)

PHONE HOME

Once there was a man who drove a big blue van,
he lived in a castle and had no hassle and he had a wonderful tan.

The man went off to work in a smart blue and red chequered shirt,
then he got sacked 'cos a cleaner he smacked
and he called his boss a berk.

The man came home in despair to find his castle wasn't there,
but in its place was a red smiling face with orange spiky hair.

'Who are you?' said the man.
'Oh I come from planet Can-Can. I have taken your home,
turned it into a phone so I can call my friend Ban Dan.'

'So what's gonna be my home now you've turned it into a phone?
Why couldn't you have gone to use a public one like everyone does
in Town Dome?'

Said the monster, 'It's your problem here, don't turn to me for ideas,
you'll just have to beat about the street; but don't come
and cry in my ear.'

So the monster, he disappeared and the man sat and scratched his beard,
there was nothing left, so he wailed and he wept.

I know it sounds awfully weird.

Chloe Barrett (12)